IDEAS IN PSYCHOANALYSIS

Phantasy

Julia Segal

Series editor: Ivan Ward

ICON BOOKS UK

TOTEM BOOKS USA

Published in the UK in 2000
by Icon Books Ltd., Grange Road,
Duxford, Cambridge CB2 4QF
email: info@iconbooks.co.uk
www.iconbooks.co.uk

Distributed in the UK, Europe,
Canada, South Africa and Asia
by the Penguin Group:
Penguin Books Ltd.,
27 Wrights Lane,
London W8 5TZ

Published in Australia in 2000
by Allen & Unwin Pty. Ltd.,
PO Box 8500, 9 Atchison Street,
St. Leonards, NSW 2065

Published in the USA in 2001
by Totem Books
Inquiries to: Icon Books Ltd.,
Grange Road, Duxford,
Cambridge CB2 4QF, UK

In the United States,
distributed to the trade by
National Book Network Inc.,
4720 Boston Way, Lanham,
Maryland 20706

Library of Congress catalog
card number applied for

ISBN 1 84046 189 6

Typesetting by Hands Fotoset

Printed and bound in the UK by
Cox & Wyman Ltd., Reading

Introduction

Why do we do what we do? Some people insist that they know the answer to this question, that everything they do is rational and sensible. These people never find themselves thinking, 'Whatever got into me?' or 'I know I shouldn't do that; why did I do it again?' – whether 'that' is drinking too much, getting involved with the wrong sort of partner, or letting their mothers upset them. Such people may not be very interested in this book. Neither will those who prefer to put things to the back of their minds for fear of opening cans of worms. However, many people find themselves doing things which take them by surprise, or which they thought they did not want to do. Some wonder what exactly the worms in those cans look like. These people may also find themselves wondering at the behaviour of others. The concept of phantasy is a tool which allows for quite subtle and complex understanding of behaviour and feelings, even though many of its ideas might initially seem ridiculous. It is only when these ideas have been observed in action that they begin to seem convincing.

The Basic Idea: Daydreams

Our perceptions of other people depend not only on their real characteristics, but also on what we bring to the relationship. For example, after we quarrel with someone, in our heads the quarrel goes on. Things are said on both sides, and our picture of the other person changes. When next we meet, we greet that person with the memory not only of what both of us actually said, but also with our interpretation of those things, as well as with the memory of the imaginary post-quarrel conversation. Our mood and that of the other will not be quite what they were when we parted; we have to find out where we stand now. Similarly, shortly after leaving home for the first time, we may start a telephone conversation with our mother, expecting her to be interested in us, our achievements, our worries – only to find that she is more interested in the neighbours, our siblings, or whatever she is doing; and in turn, she expects us to be interested in those things, too. We carry in our minds more than one picture of her. We know what she is actually like; at the same time we have a picture of the mother we would like her to be and which we somehow hope she will be.

In our heads we not only talk to people, but we also do things to and with them. In our heads we may send a bunch of flowers or a birthday card – only to be surprised when they do not actually arrive. Daydreams of friendly encounters with a pop star, perhaps, or the boy next door, merge into daydreams of sexual encounters. The other person may or may not know of these day-dreams. We may be clear about what actually happened, but sometimes we become confused between reality and imagination. Do we remember going to the seaside that year, or is it just the photograph we remember? Did our friend's father actually throw her out of the house, or just threaten to? Brothers and sisters may have quite different memories of an event, and may be angry at the construction we put on the behaviour we remember. In their heads they have worked it over differently. They may even have heard different things, since not only memory but also perception can distort. When a man says, 'You didn't tell me we were going out next weekend', he may be right; he may only have been told such a thing in his partner's fantasy. Or he may not have actually heard his partner.

These fantasies which we continually weave around our memories and experiences affect our relationship not only with the person we dream about, but also with other aspects of the world. Actually meeting someone you have fantasised about is an embarrassing idea. Anger with a friend may fade over time, or it may remain as sharp as ever. Thirty years after a bruising encounter with a life insurance salesman, a woman wrote to the Managing Director of the company concerned, saying she still felt furious with them every time their advertising literature came through the door, and would they please stop sending it? A woman who had been in a crash while in the back seat of a car could not get into another back seat for fifteen years. Being given strawberries and ice cream after tonsillitis put a child off both for twenty years.

Daydreams with Long-term Effects

Which memories or fantasies leave long-term traces and continue to annoy or distress us depends on their significance. The woman who had problems with sitting in the back seat might also have had other reasons for not wanting to 'take a back seat' metaphorically. The woman's encounter with the insurance salesman happened in the aftermath of dealing with her father's estate; powerful feelings displaced from members of her family may have played a part in elevating an ordinary instance of rudeness to a constant irritation. Strawberries and ice cream reminded the child of being miserable and alone upstairs while the family laughed below. The concept of unconscious phantasy allows us to understand how these things might happen; how we add powerfully emotive elements belonging elsewhere to a memory, and so translate it into something else: a reluctance to get into the back seat of a car; a fury at the appearance of a particular piece of advertising; a distaste for certain foods. These 'symptoms' encapsulate upsetting feelings without leading to their resolution.

Disguises

Daydreams are conscious and we can probably choose to have them or not. But less conscious fantasies go on without our awareness. We can pick these up in various ways.

A song may come into our heads for no apparent reason. With thought, we may discover the phantasies behind it. Looking out at the rain, a writer friend told me he found himself singing *'Uh oh, oh no, don't let the rain come down'*. He was puzzled, as he found it easier to write when it rains. It was only when I asked him how the song went on and he said *'My roof's got a hole in it and I might drown'*, that he remembered a roofer had told him he should do something about the state of his roof and it was worrying him. Some time later he reminded me that his mother had recently had a stroke, which he visualised as holes in her brain. I wondered if he thought he would drown in tears if she died. The 'oh no' made sense here. Tracing back from a simple snatch of song we can find anxieties which are just below the surface, expressed in concrete images. Below those, there are others. The song functioned to keep at bay both his own anxieties and (magically) his mother's death while disguising them sufficiently to allow him to work.

The concrete images are phantasies, woven together to represent and express anxieties and needs (his anxieties about his mother; his need to work). They use his experience of the present (his recent encounter with the roofer) and the past (the song itself; the belief in magic); metaphors (the 'holes' in his mother's brain); unconscious magical thinking ('I can stop my mother dying by saying "oh no"'). Phantasies in this sense are actions (a piece of magic) as well as causing actions (the refrain going through his head).

Sometimes we are aware of no more than a vague irritability in ourselves or someone else. With a bit of thought, we may be able to diagnose its cause quite easily; but we have to take that thought and there may be good reason not to. Another person may be able to see more clearly than we can.

In counselling, a woman with multiple sclerosis talked about herself and her family. I began to get a sense that she did not expect to live much longer. I asked her about this and, rather surprised, she agreed this was the case. I asked her why this might be, since my expectation would be that she would live for many more years. She did not know. I asked if her parents were still alive – puzzled, she said her father had died when he was 52; she was now 48. Suddenly she became aware that she had always thought that she was like him, and she was sure she would die at the age he had. She realised she had been unconsciously preparing for her own death for several years, and that this had affected her whole attitude towards her children and her husband. In unconscious phantasy, we can say, she was identifying with her father, and her own imminent death was a certain fact.

Fantasies which go on in our heads without our being completely aware of them can come out in other ways too. The author Martin Amis in his autobiography describes how in 1977 an ex-lover showed him a photograph of a small girl, saying it was his daughter. He gave the photo to his mother. Later he met the girl amid some publicity. Amis describes the shock which made him 'jump out of his boots' when Maureen Freely, reviewing his work, 'noted the punctual arrival – just in time for my third novel, *Success* (1978), of a stream of lost or wandering daughters and putative or fugitive fathers, and that these figures recurred, with variations, in every subsequent book'.

Amis continues:

There was nothing I could do about this

diagnosis. It chimed with something Patrick had said during our first talk on the telephone: 'I expect it's been in the back of your mind'. Yes, exactly: in the back of my mind. Your writing comes from the back of your mind, where thoughts are unformulated and anxiety is silent. I felt there was something almost embarrassing about the neatness and obviousness of the Freely interpretation. But it also sharply consoled me, because it meant that I had been with Delilah in spirit far more than I knew.[1]

Once Amis knew about the existence of his daughter, she turned up again and again in his mind – but in a disguised form. She existed in his mind in unconscious phantasy only, determining his writing without his recognising it. I think he was wrong about anxiety being silent at the back of the mind, however. We cannot silence anxieties by pushing them to the back of our minds in phantasy; we have to work them through. Until we do, they seek expression in the song which catches us unawares; in a fight we did not really mean to have; in an inhibition; in a piece of writing which others can interpret and understand.

Interpretation

It is not only novelists and psychoanalysts who interpret behaviour. We interpret other people's behaviour all the time; and sometimes those being analysed agree with us and sometimes they don't. [*'You're just like your mother!' 'You are tired.' 'I'm sorry I was bad-tempered; I was just exhausted/I was feeling hormonal/I was hungry.' 'She's bossy and a bully.' 'No, she's not. She just can't see the problem others have with doing it her way.'*]

In these interpretations we are trying to make sense of our own and other people's behaviour and feelings; the construction we put on them involves some kind of phantasy. The phantasy involves motivations and often predictions for future expectations.

Sickness involves many phantasies. [*'She caught a cold; she got very wet/everyone has a cold at the moment.' 'She was bewitched by the woman next door.' 'This lady down the road put the evil eye on her.' 'It was stress.' 'With all those children, it's not surprising she got ill.' 'She prayed to the Lord and he healed her! Praise the Lord!' 'If I exercise all the time, I won't get ill.' 'We must go to the doctor/priest/shaman and ask him to find out what is wrong with her.' 'Every time his father went away, he got a chest infection.' 'It's all in the mind.' 'Whatever is wrong with me, I know it is NOT my mind; it is my BODY.'*]

These interpretations are explanations which can influence behaviour. They deal with the powerful anxiety of not knowing what caused misfortune and what we can expect to happen next. Phantasies serve to contain anxieties by giving us explanations, often based on little evidence. Some allow for questions and answers; others do not.

Illness and death are both interruptions to normal life. They shake a set of phantasies that rely on the assumption that tomorrow we will be much the same as we are today. We do not think, 'Tomorrow I will not have flu'; we just assume it will be the case. We assume we will go on living for the foreseeable future, or we may have a vague or a clear idea about when we expect to die – and this is very unlikely to be 'tomorrow'. These assumptions are embodied in the normal phantasies we have which prepare us to face the world when we wake up. In these phantasies we know, without thinking about it, what our bodies are doing, what our mind is like, what they will do for us tomorrow. We may get angry and upset when these normal phantasies are challenged. When flu or some other illness intervenes, it takes us unawares and we have to rearrange the phantasies on which we base our normal life. Phantasies encapsulate normal assumptions about the world. We become aware of them, if at all, when they no longer fit and we have to seek new ones.

The Freudian Background

Freud discovered phantasies when he began

trying to understand various symptoms as a neurologist. Nowadays we would call these 'conversion symptoms': they convert an idea into a phobia or an apparently medical symptom which the doctors cannot explain. For example, in examining a woman who said she had no sensation in her arm, Freud found that the lack of feeling followed the sleeve area, rather than nerve pathways. He also found that he could replicate loss of sensation or movement with hypnosis. From this came the realisation that ideas and thoughts could control the body in a way which was completely unconscious. He found that by allowing patients to 'free associate', he could build a picture of the ideas at the back of their minds which explained the symptoms. Like Amis, his patients often did not like these ideas.

One case involved a young man who had to run back along the road and move a stone for fear that his fiancée's carriage would hit it and there would be an accident. By some tortuous reasoning, he then had to go and put the stone back in the road.[2] As Freud listened to the young man talk, it became clear that he was terrified of killing his fiancée, but at the same time he wanted her hurt or even dead. This idea was deeply disguised from the young man himself, and he had no idea it was affecting his behaviour.

Freud at first thought that it was unbearable memories which were converted into symptoms; eventually he came to realise that the root causes were fantasies, memories encapsulated in stories, of events which might or might not have taken place. As everyone knows, he found young girls with fantasies of having sex with their fathers and young men with fantasies of having sex with their mothers. Both sexes also had fantasies of killing their parents. None of them actually thought consciously, 'I have tried to kill my father' or 'I have had sex with my father'. Like any sensible person would, they rejected the idea.

I became convinced of the reality of these ideas only after several mothers I knew told me of their small sons getting upset at the realisation that they could not marry their mothers or 'have babies in their wombs'. Now adults, these boys deny all memory of this humiliating idea.

Freud's patients' symptoms functioned both to express and to fend off the thought (just as the 'Uh oh, oh no' song expressed and fended off the thought of the mother's death). Freud found that he needed a new concept to distinguish unconscious phantasy (rejected from conscious thought but having an effect 'from the back of the mind', where the patient was unaware of it) from conscious fantasies (such as daydreams). It was James Strachey, Freud's translator, who decided to use the 'ph' spelling to distinguish conscious from unconscious fantasy, in order to clarify a complex situation.[3]

Phantasy, then, was understood at first as a fantasy of an event such as killing one's father or having sex with him, which appeared to pre-occupy a certain group of disturbed individuals and caused mental, or apparently physical, illness. These fantasies were never conscious, and when they became conscious they lost their power to create symptoms.

In 'Studies in Hysteria', Freud wrote up a series of cases which make fascinating reading. Fräulein Elizabeth von R. came to Freud with leg pains that had no neurological explanation. She agreed to allow Freud to try his 'talking cure', but after months of talking to Freud about whatever came into her mind, she was horrified to discover that the pains represented a form of self-flagellation for incestuous feelings towards her brother-in-law. Once the idea had become conscious, the physical pains went away (and so did she), though for a long time they were replaced with painful thoughts. Freud describes the case thus:

The recovery of this repressed idea had a shattering effect on the poor girl. She cried aloud when I put the situation drily before her with the words: 'So for a long time you had been in love with your brother-in-law.' She complained at this moment of the most frightful pains, and made one last desperate effort to reject the explanation: it was not true, I had talked her into it, it could not be true, she was incapable of such wickedness, she could never forgive herself for it. It was easy to prove to her that what she herself had told me admitted of no other interpretation. But it was a long time before my two pieces of consolation – that we are not responsible for our feelings, and that her behaviour, the fact that she had fallen ill in these circumstances, was sufficient evidence of her moral character – it was a long time before these consolations of mine made any impression on her.[4]

Freud said that the girl's mother had known about her daughter's feelings towards her brother-in-law for a long time. Part of the humiliation of uncovering aspects of ourselves we thought were well hidden can be the discovery that others have not been fooled, only ourselves.

Dreams

In his attempts to elucidate the thoughts and memories which lay behind symptoms, Freud found himself being told dreams. In dreams, the 'censor' which kept ideas out of consciousness worked differently, and the disguises were easier to penetrate.

He described a young woman whose illness

began with a state of confusional excitement during which she displayed a quite special aversion to her mother, hitting and abusing her whenever she came near her bed, while at the same period she was docile and affectionate towards a sister who was many years her senior. This was followed by a period in which she was lucid but somewhat apathetic and suffered from badly disturbed sleep. It was during this phase that I began treating her and analysing her dreams. An immense number of these dreams were concerned, with a greater or less degree of disguise, with the death of her mother: at one time she would be attending an old woman's funeral, at another she and her sister would be sitting at table dressed in mourning. There could be no question as to the meaning of these dreams. As her condition improved still further, hysterical phobias developed. The most tormenting of these was a fear that something might have happened to her mother. She was obliged to hurry home, wherever she might be, to convince herself that her mother was still alive.[5]

Freud saw this case as demonstrating the different ways in which hostility to the woman's mother was expressed, as physical aggression or symbolised in a dream, or defended against by the conscious substitution of the opposite idea as a negation.

It was in the analysis of mental disturbances, then, that Freud discovered symbolism, which he found often linked to disturbing sexual fantasies. When he examined Elizabeth von R.'s painful legs by pinching them, she did not react as someone in pain; instead *her face assumed a peculiar expression, which was one of pleasure rather than pain. She cried out – and I could not help thinking that it was as though she was having a voluptuous tickling sensation – her faced flushed, she threw back her head and shut her eyes and her body bent backwards . . . Her expression . . . was probably more in harmony with the subject-matter of the thoughts which lay concealed behind the pain.*[6]

A region of her legs had come to represent some aspect of her sexuality. Later Freud discovered that this was an area which had touched her father's swollen leg while she nursed him as he lay dying. Freud thought we symbolised only things which we did not want to know about, which were repressed, and that these repressed thoughts came out in symptoms. As in the case of Elizabeth von R., the symptoms were over-determined; many unconscious thoughts or fantasies lay behind each one. But Freud saw the symptomatic leg and other symbols as existing in a world of more neutral objects which had no particular psychic significance.

Klein: Children's Play

Melanie Klein was a mother of young children when she read Freud's *Interpretation of Dreams* (1900). Watching her own son playing, making mountains out of her body and running his carriages and people over it; listening to him relating his fantasies about his 'wiwi' and 'making babies' with his 'poo'; telling the paper he wiped himself with to 'eat it up', she realised that she could interpret his play and his stories as Freud interpreted dreams. In 'The Development of a Child', she gives a wealth of examples of her son's fantasies.[7] For example, 'the womb figured as a completely furnished house, the stomach particularly was very fully equipped and was even possessed of a bath-tub and a soap-dish. He remarked himself: "I know it isn't really like that, but I see it that way"'.[8]

Freud had begun to think that it was repression of sexual interest which kept phantasies out of conscious awareness and therefore liable to emerge as symptoms, so Klein decided she would try to bring her son up without this repression. She decided to tell him where babies came from. This was revolutionary at the time, and it is not surprising that she could not quite bring herself to explain about the role of the father: besides, the child did not ask. This led to an important discovery. Her son was interested in what she said, but after a while he began asking stereotyped questions about what different things were made of and how they were made. For instance, 'What is a door made of? – What is the bed made of ? . . . How does all the earth get under the earth? . . . Where do stones, where does water come from? . . .' Klein explained that 'There was no doubt that . . . he had completely grasped the answer to these questions and that their recurrence had no intellectual basis. He showed too by his inattentive and absent-minded behaviour while putting the questions that he was really indifferent about the answers in spite of the fact that he asked them with vehemence . . .'[9] When she saw him gradually losing interest in everything, including being told stories by her, she remembered that a senior analyst had pointed out that the boy was asking about the role of the father in a disguised form. After she explained it to him, the child completely regained his interest in the world, began to play freely and to relate stories to her.[10]

She began to analyse her own children (though she warned her pupils later against doing this, feeling it was too intrusive), then other children and later, adults. Klein, like Freud, began to see that unconscious phantasies could have powerful effects on daily life. Her own son's temporary inhibition had been cured by her answering an unconscious question, and she found other children with symptoms, who also responded to analysis of their play and speech. Her son had shown her evidence of considerable aggression towards his brother, sister and father; for example, in a game where he cut off their heads;[11] but he later became anxious about these games. Klein realised that it was not just negative adult attitudes towards sexual ideas which could cause children to inhibit their interests or to change their games, but their own internal conflicts, in particular about their fantasies of damaging or destroying those they loved.

A child called 'Fritz', described in 'The Role of the School in the Libidinal Development of the Child', had many difficulties at school, including an inhibition to doing division sums. Klein says that 'Fritz'

told me that in doing division he had first of all to bring down the figure that was required and he climbed up, seized it by the arm and pulled it down. To my enquiry as to what it said to that, he replied that quite certainly it was not pleasant for the number – it was as if his mother stood on a stone 13 yards high and someone came and caught her by the arm so that they tore it out and divided her. . . . He then related . . . that actually every child wants to have a bit of his mother, who is to be cut in four pieces; he depicted quite exactly how she screamed and had paper stuffed in her mouth so that she could not scream, and what kind of faces she made, etc. A child took a very sharp knife, and he described how she was cut up; first across the width of the breast, and then of the belly, then lengthwise so that the 'pipi' [in his imagination, mothers also had penises, it seems], *the face and the head were cut exactly through the middle, whereby the 'sense' was taken out of her head. The head was then again cut through obliquely just as the 'pipi' was cut across its breadth. Betweenwhiles he constantly bit at his hand and said that he bit his sister too for fun, but certainly for love. He continued that every child then took the piece of the mother that it wanted, and agreed that the cut-up mother was then also eaten. It now appeared also that he always confused the remainder with the quotient in division, and always wrote it in the wrong place, because in his mind it was bleeding pieces of flesh with which he was unconsciously dealing. These inter-*

pretations completely removed his inhibition with regard to division.[12]

In a note, Klein adds: 'The next day in school to his and his mistress's astonishment, it turned out that he could now do all his sums correctly. (The child had not become aware of the connection between the interpretation and the removal of the inhibition.)'

Klein had discovered that children create frightening phantasies based on misunderstandings of the world fuelled by their anxieties. Uncovering these phantasies could reduce the fear and free children to use their minds fully and creatively. Klein says of her son:

To begin with, before he starts relating things he enquires quite cheerfully whether what he finds 'horrid' will, after I have explained it to him, become pleasant again for him just as with the other things so far. He also says that he is not afraid any more of the things that have been explained to him even when he thinks of them.[13]

Klein's new insights turned Freud's upside down. She saw that we endow the world and everything in it with meaning derived from unconscious phantasies and the anxieties which lie behind these. It is our anxieties, our conflicting impulses and the derived phantasies which lead us to see the things we see and behave in the way we do. In this sense, nothing is neutral. In phantasy all kinds of things are going on, in our heads, in our bodies, in our 'inner world'. We do not always know it 'isn't really like that'; we really do 'see it that way'. The pains in Elizabeth's legs were real for her and really blotted out her 'immoral' thoughts for a while. 'Fritz's' phantasy about division sums was so convincing that it stopped him doing them. People who believe in witchcraft are really frightened by it. And it is possible that the real atrocities of war which so frighteningly mirror some of the children's phantasies described by Klein are caused by people acting on infantile phantasies in which people are closer to terrifying monsters or things than to human beings.

Phantasies as Perception

We can now look at unconscious phantasies from a different point of view. Klein discovered that phantasies provide the basic tools we use to make sense of our perceptions. They create the basic assumptions we use to live by; affecting not just disturbed behaviour, but also ordinary, everyday behaviour. Sensations of all kinds, arising from inside or outside ourselves, are all interpreted through phantasies. Phantasies also motivate perception. Seeking confirmation of our goodness or badness, we find people and situations which will tell us we are good or bad.

Work is motivated as much by unconscious phantasies about making things in the world better as by the more conscious ones of needing the money. ('The world', like the mountains in Klein's son's play, often stands for some idea of an early phantasy of the mother, with or without the father, who once made up our world.) Even conscious motivations have unconscious roots. If we take seriously what people say when they lose their jobs, it seems that 'money' can represent their own value to themselves and others, as well as their life, potency, the capacity to take care of loved people, or even proof that they are not the failure their father always said, for example. In phantasy, 'money' may be endowed with all these meanings, and the reassurance and comfort that it brings as it comes in every week or month may be enormous. Likewise, the ordinary behaviour of seeking a lover is clearly governed by unconscious phantasies about what he or she will do for you, and what you will do for him or her. Not all of these are realistic. The details of names, ages, physical, emotional and mental characteristics of a partner are also all likely to resonate with those of family members. Phantasies derived from the earliest family situation create a basis on which people encountered subsequently are then met, welcomed, understood or rejected accordingly.

'Fritz's' dislike of long division is thus perhaps 'disturbed', but it is a common disturbance. His phantasies endowed his division sums with horror. When his mother was away, his need to deal with his anger against her (for abandoning him) created phantasies of a witch who might poison him. These phantasies were separate from the mother he loved and wanted back. Children do often behave badly after their parents have been away for any reason; it makes sense that there might be ordinary angry phantasies behind this behaviour.

Phantasies motivate and underlie ordinary play. Hormonal surges and external frustrations create anger, which is perceived through phantasies which then govern its expression. Ball and computer games allow violent phantasies safe expression, well away from any idea of wanting to kill a real person. (But ask for names of the combatants in a computer game and there may be a hint of an underlying phantasy.) Playing these games modifies the phantasies available to understand and control reactions the next time anger arises. Girls' play often expresses strong feelings and phantasies about 'insides and out-sides', for example through making and breaking circles of friendship, rope or beads.

Children also make sense of their parents' behaviour by using their own experience, coloured by their anxieties and needs. A boy of twelve talked about how angry he was with his father for not helping in the house; he said he was lazy for not doing his fair share; why should he help if his father did not? The boy knew his father was ill, but he had no understanding of neurological fatigue. In his phantasy, his father was motivated as he would be himself. I do not think it was pure self-interest which motivated this boy, but a much deeper anxiety about his father's illness. I suspect that he did not want to think of his father as unable to do things, as ill, weak and vulnerable; it was far preferable to think of him as strong and resistant to his mother's demands – as the boy would have liked to be himself.

Basic expectations of the wider world develop from the earliest phantasies created out of the child's interpretations of his or her childhood world. For example, as a child, Sue took it for granted that women always told men what to do, because that was how it was in her extended family. It was quite a shock when she went to school and discovered that nurses (female) had to do what doctors (male) told them. In another instance, Frances's father left home when she was two and a half years old. Several sexual relationships throughout her twenties and early thirties lasted almost exactly two and a half years. Frances did not think that there was any connection and was annoyed when I suggested there might be.

The phantasies we use to understand our own children are also based on our phantasies about ourselves and our parents. We may see our children as stupid and ignorant as we always feared we were; or we might see them as able to fulfil our wildest dreams. We may love them as we feel that we loved our parents. We may fear that they want to punish us, as we wanted to punish our parents. Parents often seem to have fantasies of being worn out, or done to death by their own children, and not only when they are ill. A woman told her grandson that he would kill his mother by breastfeeding: 'You'll suck her dry, you know!' And of course, the Oedipus story is scary from the point of view of the adults in it.

Primitive Phantasies

The most primitive phantasies, we think, are there at birth. Babies are born with a capacity to recognise certain objects and to react in certain ways. They actively seek the breast and nipple, by smell, feel, recognition of the mother's voice and reacting to a dark spot in a lighter circle. When they find the nipple, they know what to do, though there may be a few false starts. A phantasy corresponding to nipple-in-the-mouth seeks something in the outside world to match it. The experience of being fed then modifies this phantasy, so that very soon it has to involve the mother's own familiar nipple, with the right voice, smell and feel attached to it.

The modification of phantasies continues throughout life, so that later experiences of eating may seem to bear little resemblance to the first feed; later experiences of loving and being loved may not appear to have much in common with the tiny baby's love affair with the mother's breast, or the older baby's wordless adoration of a bigger sibling. But a connecting thread leads from one to another, and sometimes it is possible to see. A baby who always grabbed the nipple with enthusiasm, almost biting it but not quite, may be recognisable in an adult who greets new experiences energetically, getting her teeth into them in a similar way. Another adult who always holds back suspiciously, who does not quite trust the world, may have greeted his or her first feeds in much the same way. Underlying assumptions about the world may create phantasies which remain active many years later, regardless of actual experience.

Another thread connects all good experiences with each other. Good sex has something in common with a good feed, even in adulthood; also with a good conversation, a jazz or rock concert, or even a good book. The underlying phantasies are derived from the same basic ones; later distortions have not completely done away with the connection. The baby at the breast having a good feed has a whole-body experience of pleasure; its skin is flushed, its mouth wonderfully full; it is held in bliss for a timeless moment; nothing must interrupt. The experience has a beginning (when the baby must work hard to start the milk flowing); it has a middle (when the sucking is long and slow and rhythmic); and it has an end (when the baby falls off the breast with a drunken look of pleasure). What is more, such pleasure is not easily won; it arises only (if at all) after mother and child have learned how to do it. Pain, difficulty, discomfort and awkwardness often accompany the first experiences at the breast, as well as the first experiences of penetrative sex. The parallels are clear (to me, anyway), and extend to other experiences. The rhythm and structure of a conversation, for example, can also reflect good or bad sex. It may be boring, never coming to the point, or exciting. It may reach a climax and leave a satisfied feeling, giving rise to creative thoughts; or it may be crude, brutal and short, leaving a bad taste in the mouth. The word 'intercourse' refers both to 'sexual union' and 'conversation', just as the word 'conversation' also used to have both meanings.

The structure of a phantasy used in creating a conversation, a piece of music, a meal, or a story may have its roots in the earliest pleasurable phantasies, long forgotten but still leaving discernible traces. Phantasies are more primitive than thought. They provide the mental representations of our experiences and needs; they define the assumptions we use to understand and make sense of our world *without having to think about it*. A small baby does not *think*, for example, 'that pain inside me is hunger'; it simply starts looking for food.

Hunger Phantasies

The example of hunger is a useful one. Adults do not in fact always start looking for food when they are hungry; they may decide to wait a while. The baby may only appear to be seeking food. In phantasy it may be seeking anything to fill a phantasy gap, to smother or to punish the phantasy biting monsters inside, or to hold onto until the biting stops. Adults may start looking for food when it is in fact the pain of loss, misery or anger which is hurting inside. Phantasies about eating are often unrealistic, or connected with experiences which are not just hunger for food.

A younger sister may choose what she eats by watching her bigger sister or brother, rather than responding to her own appetite. In phantasy she is perhaps being them, with their appetite, not her own. Another person may in phantasy use food to stuff down a dependent, miserable, weak, lonely child part of the self and prevent it howling. Hunger may evoke a phantasy of a fat, intrusive mother pushing food at her daughter, saying 'Come on, dear, you must eat', bringing instant revulsion. Or hunger pangs may be interpreted as guilt, so the search for food is complicated by needing to clean up first, or to choose 'self-denying' foods. Hunger may bring feelings about a lost father who smoked; so a cigarette allows a comforting phantasy of breathing him in with the tobacco smoke, while smothering the anger for his unexpected departure and keeping the body slim as he liked it. On the other hand, one woman insisted on eating butter in large quantities, because, she said, it meant the war was over: during the war she had always given her butter ration to her mother, and she never intended to give it up again. And so on. The phantasies governing food, drink and smoking are enormously complex. (Susie Orbach describes some phantasies to do with eating in her book *Fat is a Feminist Issue*.[14])

Many phantasies distort truth, telling us we are not hungry when we are, or that we are happy when we are not, for example. They distort our view of ourselves and our own feelings [*'I'm not jealous.'* *'Everything I do is bad.'* *'I am the wrong sex.'*]. They also distort our view of our children [*'He hasn't noticed his father's absence.'* *'She was such a good girl.'*].

Importance of Truth

Whether our phantasies are close to reality or a

long way short of it matters. The closer our phantasies come to reality, the less likely we are to be suddenly brought up short against facts that do not fit. However, just as there may be strong emotional reasons for holding onto unrealistic worldviews, so there are plenty of 'stories' we can tell ourselves to 'explain' discrepancies in our view of the world and others' (e.g., 'They are stupid'; or 'They are unbelievers and will go to hell'; or 'They don't really know me; if they did they would *know* I am really very bad/good'). Certain phantasies represent illusions about the world which are shared with others, and our acquiescence with these makes us more or less comfortable in our social world. For example, in a world with extremes of poverty and riches, we may seek justification for our own position relative to others in order to be able to function without a constant sense of guilt towards those less fortunate. However, if this involves in phantasy 'shutting our eyes' to what we know are injustices, it gives us blind spots which may have other consequences.

Klein believed that our relation to the truth was vitally important. She found that even uncomfortable reality was in the long term preferable to trying to live in an illusory phantasy-world; the phantasies we use to confuse ourselves, to pretend that the world is closer to our wishes than it really is, were all damaging in one way or another. Not only did they damage our capacity to see and feel and think truthfully, but they also threatened our relations with other people and ourselves. Attempts to hide a painful idea from ourselves do not remain static; they draw to themselves other ideas or thoughts which might remind us of the idea; we have to 'forget' those too; before long we can end up unable to take an interest in anything for fear it will lead to the painful idea.

Many people disagree with Klein about this, claiming that illusion can be better in many ways than reality. Those who watch soap operas or go to church are apparently happier in some measurable way than those who do not. I suspect that the conscious and unconscious fantasy worlds these supply have much to recommend them for many people. I also suspect that they often fail at certain points when they are really needed, such as at times of illness. The characters from *Neighbours* do not deliver hot meals when you need them, whereas real neighbours may bring more conflicts but real food. And as a counsellor for people with multiple sclerosis, I have found that many religious beliefs fail to provide comfort when people have an illness which does not get better.

My own experience has convinced me that Klein was right; but it is vital to remember how difficult she thought it was to recognise truth when we see it. I know how painful and humiliating truth can be; and it may not be my place to expose it, even if I am convinced I can see it. Giving painful information, for example, requires patience, time and understanding; one cannot just 'drop it and run'. I would need to be sure I could offer real substitutes for the many pleasures of soap operas or religion before trying to undermine them in an adult; with my own children I have more choices about what I offer in the way of explanations and pleasures in life.

To return to phantasies governing eating, it is clear that some unrealistic phantasies may result in good, normal eating, but many will not. In a similar way, unrealistic phantasies about the end of the world may result in social policies that help protect the environment; and Columbus's phantasies about the existence of a passage to India and the glory of God resulted in a journey to the West Indies. Other phantasies about God, however, bring holy wars, death and destruction of one kind or another.

Phantasies in Action

I want now briefly to look at some of the significant phantasies we use.

Phantasies of the Good Object

Some of the most important phantasies involve what Klein called the good object. She was talking about phantasies of a good, loving, holding, containing figure inside, available for comfort and for comforting communication. The mother-in-your-head who loves you and understands you and wants the best for you is a good object; so is a good father-figure. Analysts use the word 'object' here to mean 'not the subject'; i.e., 'not-me'; someone/thing who is generally bigger or stronger in some way; providing something that the self cannot provide for itself. As the child grows, phantasies of the good object change and grow too.

Not everyone has a sense of a solid, reliable good object. Premature independence which creates a 'false self', for example, can result from a phantasy of a good object which is unsafe and unreliable and which needs to be looked after by an immature self.

Phantasies of Being Merged

The earliest phantasies seem to include an awareness of someone/thing who is 'not me' and a desire to join up with this figure. The first rooting for the nipple is a search for something;

but is that something outside the self, or something necessary to complete the self? Plato's story depicting men and women as originally one male/female, torn apart and forever seeking our 'other half' or 'better half' implies a phantasy of the good object which combines both self and other. It is not surprising if boundaries between the baby self and the mother are not clear, but adults too can have difficulty knowing where they begin and their partner or their mother or father ends. Close couples sometimes 'know' what the other is thinking or feeling, without words; 'talking for' a child or a partner implies some phantasy of being one, which the other may or may not appreciate. Loving sexual relationships often involve fantasies of merging, becoming one, uniting against the world, making an indissoluble bond. However, there is a difference between merging into one and bonding as two separate beings.

Being merged with the loved object brings difficulties. Parts of the self which are different from the other may begin to feel trapped, stifled. These phantasies have their effects on the external world, and the loved person too may feel excessively controlled. Phantasies of being merged with another can be found in babies, their mothers and in some adult relationships. Where these lead to phantasies of being stifled, they can even provoke asthma attacks. Recognising the loved good object as someone separate not only allows each to breathe; it also allows for feelings of love and concern freely given. In the case of some couples who think that they want a divorce, what they really need is to separate in their heads; the separation in reality may then not be necessary.

For example, a woman told me she could not live with her husband any more. He watched every step she took; he wouldn't even let her buy knickers without his permission. I asked her how this worked; did she not have her own money? No, she had her own money; it was just that she knew he would disapprove. And how did she know this? Did he tell her? No, in fact, he never said anything; she just knew how he felt. It gradually became clear that he was so constantly present in her mind in fantasy that she never felt the need to ask him what he actually thought about anything. She just '*knew*'. When I cautiously pointed this out, she was quite startled. I was curious to know if she would ask him or not about her buying knickers. The next time I saw her, she was astonished to report that now it had been sorted out; he had no objection to her buying knickers at all; he was less bothered about how she spent money than she was. She had had no idea about his true feelings. It seemed that the person who felt she should not buy knickers was herself, but with her husband's encouragement she was able to go and choose some that she really liked, for the first time in her life.

The woman did not want to leave her husband after all. The phantasy of having him inside her, watching over her and identified with a restrictive part of her, had changed to one in which she could bear to see him as different, outside her, needing to communicate in words. Disentangling herself from her husband in her mind enabled her to begin to live with a real husband who was different from her and who brought her things she could not give herself – including permission to enjoy herself. Both could now live and love each other without, in her phantasy, being completely confused with each other.

Fathers play an important role in helping babies and children to separate from their mothers. Mothers have to identify with the baby initially in order to understand what it needs, but this identification can become frightening for both mother and child. In phantasy as well as reality, fathers come between mother and baby, preventing them from stifling each other, allowing the mother to regain a sense of herself as an adult and the baby to relate to a different person in a different way. Just as the baby wants to merge with its mother, so in the baby's phantasy, its parents are sometimes allowed to merge with each other, and, when this feels painful, to be separated again. Adults are often confused about the differences between their parents, as if they have never quite separated them out correctly. And people with schizophrenia sometimes fear merging in a very concrete way. They may fear that they will get totally tangled up with another person, literally falling inside them, for example.

Giving Parts of the Self

When we love someone, we want to give him or her things: food, love, books to read, films to watch. In phantasy (as in love songs) we give our selves to those we love. We also give them parts of ourselves, not just our heart. We want to join our bodies, if only temporarily, in sexual acts. We may want to give them babies or have their babies or create something together such as songs or works of art. In phantasy we may give them our own capacities too. For example, they may be more optimistic or generous than we are; and we may be happy to let them be optimistic or generous for us too. After a time, however, it may seem that they never see the more pessimistic side of things; they never worry about money, leaving us alone with our fears for a joint future. Or they may be able to earn more money, and we may be happy to give up our job and let them take responsibility for earning; again, after a while this bargain may not seem so comfortable, especially if earning money seems to carry with it higher social esteem, or permission never to cook another meal or wash another dish. Equally, our loved ones may give us parts of themselves: the more-responsible-with-money part; or the thinking-about-the-children part; or the driving-the-car part, or the filling-in-forms or dealing-with-authorities part. In phantasy we can chop ourselves up into many parts and pass them around, as 'Fritz' did with his mother every time he was faced with a long division sum.

Sometimes in phantasy we give of ourselves out of love, or for safe keeping, or in hope of increasing everyone's happiness. Sometimes these phantasies are more cruel or desperate, however. We may give parts of ourselves to others to control them or hurt them or to save our own life at the expense of theirs. Ambitious women are sometimes accused of handing over their own ambition to a husband, chasing the husband to fulfil their ambitions and then complaining when he does not do it well enough. Marrying someone who likes to feel better than everyone else may enable a woman (or man) to get rid of her or his own sense of superiority safely for a while. But it may eventually lead to being treated with contempt by the husband (or wife). Equally, loading a lover with one's own sense of inferiority or badness or uselessness or impotence allows the self to feel superior. In phantasy there may be a fear that the other has been expected to hold too much; that he or she may have been filled up with too much of our anger, contempt or hatred. Fear of losing the good object sometimes arises from such phantasies.

If these transactions have been basically loving, we feel that a good object can survive, our fears of losing it are reduced, and we can feel that it is strong and resilient. The good object helps put us back together, not allowing us to lose touch entirely with our own capacities, encouraging us to develop aspects of ourselves we did not know before, and helping us to survive the knocks of life. In reasonably happy circumstances this is what our parents, united as a couple, did in our earliest phantasies, and what a partner, parent, close friend or child may do later in life. Our worst moments may be when we fear we have lost this good object, represented by any of these people. Because the good object contains much of ourselves, we can feel that we are falling apart and losing ourselves at the same time.

The Bad Object; Bad Parents; Bad Lovers; Bad Babies; the Bad Self

The development of the good object takes place in parallel with phantasies of a threatening bad one. Initially, when the good mother is not there the baby may simply feel the presence of a bad one. When parents are downstairs laughing, a child may sometimes lie in bed fearing the witch or the burglar under the bed, the spider or the scary daddy-long-legs on the wall, until a (real) parent is sought to banish it. Over time, the child may allow itself to be aware that it is angry with the parents for being downstairs together and may not need to create frightening monsters out of secret fury. This becomes easier as the child is able to make its own life which can exclude the parents. People outside the family can take on good and bad parent aspects.

Bad objects can also be created out of an attempt to idealise a good one. Those aspects which are not liked can be separated off in phantasy and attributed to someone else. A young adult may blame all his or her troubles on one parent and see the other as a helpless victim. The victim is supposedly loved and the oppressor hated; but actually the supposedly loved parent is diminished and reduced in phantasy, and in reality, patronised. (To be a victim means to be weak; collusion or manipulation of the other parent by the victim may be ignored.) Idealisation is often a defence against phantasies of persecution: the persecuting, bad, angry aspects of the supposed good parent are attributed to the supposed bad one who can then be hated with impunity. 'My mother would have taken more notice of me if my father had let her' has an implication that she is completely at his mercy. 'My father was a good, kind, sweet man; but my mother drove him to drink.' 'My mother was an angel and my father a devil.' Relationships are seldom this simple; the angel might turn out to be a devil in disguise. The 'can of worms' that people fear if they begin to unpick their childhood memories sometimes turns out to contain the shocking realisation that an angelic parent was not so angelic, and a devil parent perhaps guiltily and distressingly maligned.

As the child becomes a young adult, girlfriends and boyfriends can take the place of parents in terms of providing a reference group, and creating their own definitions of reality which may be different from those of the parents. Young adults may seek good objects, or they may seek bad ones, as lovers. Bad ones provide containment for unbearable bad aspects of the self and may be comforting in this way. Ultimately they may prove a great threat to the self; but if this self is at depth felt to be bad in phantasy, the threat may be welcomed as a deserved punishment. Dangerous or bullying lovers may also be felt to punish the parents inside. Real parents, of course, are also made to suffer when their son or daughter is in a bad relationship.

In good circumstances, phantasies of perfect parents, destroyed when they fail to live up to perfection, are replaced by more ordinary ones which can survive disappointment. Gradually the child stops wanting to kill the evil mother-who-is-not-there but can hold on to a phantasy of a loving mother who survives absences.

Functions of Phantasy: Dealing with Conflicts

There are many ways of dealing with conflicts in phantasy. An internal struggle can take place; do I do this, or do I do that? A conflict can also be externalised. Two people with the same internal conflict can argue with each other rather than inside their own heads. One may be arguing that he can do something; the other says he cannot. The internal conflict has been split between them and can be played out in the outside world. Sometimes the issue is close to the underlying unconscious conflict; sometimes it only represents it. For example, one partner may claim to want more sex and the other less, neither wanting to admit to any ambivalence over the subject. Some couples can have this fight; others may translate it into arguments about money or about time spent together, or about football or nights out with friends, any of which may be disguised ways of expressing anxieties connected to the question of whether they love each other or not.

Conflicts can also be dealt with in stories. A small girl has to cope with her conflicts over loving her mother and at the same time envying all her possessions and attributes, as well as her ability to tell the child what to do, to demand help from her, and to leave her behind while the mother goes out and has a good time. In addition, the girl may suffer terrible jealousy over the love her parents bear for each other and for their other children. There are many ways of dealing with this conflict in phantasy. Some girls deny that their parents love each other and in phantasy hold on to a belief that it is only they who are loved. Some deny that they want their parents to love them, and try to develop a 'don't care' attitude. They may seek the love they want in premature sexual relationships which are doomed to failure because they are based not on love of the parents, but revenge against them, which eventually re-emerges in revenge on the lover.

Most little girls end up with some form of coming to terms with their own mixed feelings towards their parents. The Cinderella story represents a phantasy in which the small girl can try out many mixed feelings towards her parents without having to see clearly what she is doing. Stories like this may be understood like computer games, as a means of children externalising and playing out conflicts and anxieties in a safe setting.

Cinderella's mother is split into a good (but dead) mother and a bad (but living) stepmother. Both are idealised and unrealistic. Reading the story, in phantasy identifying with Cinderella, a small girl can enjoy the pleasure of triumphing over a (step) mother who has beautiful clothes, daughters of her own and the love of the girl's father, while denying that this mother is the same one as the mother she loves. The ugly, envious feelings a real little girl cannot avoid when contemplating her mother's and older siblings' possessions are attributed to the ugly sisters when, at the end of the story, it is Cinderella who is the object of envy and admiration.

Phantasies of Splitting the Mother Mean Splitting the Self

The Cinderella story shows how phantasies of splitting the object – the real mother – can be experienced as deadly: the good mother is dead but Cinderella has no responsibility for this. The reader identified with Cinderella in phantasy has no guilt to bear. Phantasies of splitting the good mother from the bad one also involve splitting the self. The dead mother/stepmother split is reflected in the split between Cinderella and her stepsisters, but Cinderella herself is split again into the beautiful princess and the ragged girl who come together at the end of the story. The pairing of the shoes at the end also hints at Cinderella's need to bring two parts of herself/ her object together. It suggests, perhaps, that the little girl will be able to bring these parts of herself together when she is old enough to have her own husband.

Phantasies of splitting the self can explain why we sometimes do things which take us by surprise; the 'me' which behaves like that is not one 'I' recognise as myself – or not one I want to recognise as me. Because splitting takes place unconsciously, it can be a real shock to recognise a split-off part of the self; as Amis did when he realised he had been writing about his daughter in a disguised form for years. It seems that the part of him which cared and was concerned and perhaps curious had been hidden from the self he knew.

Much of the work of counselling and psycho-analysis involves clarifying and mending splits in the self, bringing together aspects of the self in such a way that concern, love and reparative capacities are freer to express themselves without being swamped by phantasies of revenge or anger or destruction.

Denial

The phantasy that something can simply be ignored and then it will go away has many forms. 'Positive thinking' may mean consciously replacing happy thoughts for unhappy ones. The unhappy ones are then pushed under the carpet or 'stuffed down a well'. In phantasy the thoughts may be cut out, chopped to bits; we can shut the door on them, refuse to go down that road. Our language is full of hints about the kinds of phantasies we use [*No way! You must be joking! I won't countenance it! I don't know what got into me. It wasn't like her.*]. These last two imply phantasies in which some trouble-some behaviour is acknowledged but ownership is somehow questioned. Some people *cocoon themselves; cut themselves off; hide under the bedclothes; roll up in a ball and shut their eyes tight; bury their heads in the sand.* They may use drink *to drown their sorrows.* In phantasy the drowned 'sorrows' are personified, perhaps as a small, dependent and miserable child self, or a vicious, uncaring, accusing adult bad object. The drink may represent debased milk or what 'Fritz' called 'wiwi'; alcohol in such phantasies is poison rather than good food.

The problem with all of these is that the unwanted thoughts remain in their original state and are not brought into contact with reality which can modify them. They remain active 'at the back of the mind'. A phantasy of the lover felt as uncaring, 'driving to drink', is not checked against reality but remains seen through an ancient phantasy of an uncaring parent or an uncaring self.

Denial can be helped along in other ways too. It is not so easy to *really* 'not see' what is there; something has to be done to the perception. One common way of dealing with it is to 'see' it elsewhere, to thrust it in phantasy into or onto a different person. For example, a car driver waiting at a roundabout pulls out into a bicycle coming off the roundabout in front of him. The car driver shouts at the cyclist that she should watch where she is going. Clearly his perception that *someone* should watch where he or she is going is accompanied by a powerful 'Not me!' Denial of reality can often be helped along by focusing on something different. The bad behaviour of other people, particularly on the road, is a useful source of aggrieved feelings which for some people can be relied on to keep their attention off what they have done themselves. This driver probably went away swearing at cyclists. This is also an example of an attack used as a defence. Attacking, demanding punishment, and blame can all be used to help along denial; in particular, denial of guilt.

In phantasy we do not always distinguish one person from another. Just as in dreams a person may be one moment our father, the next a teacher or ex-lover, the next a husband or son, so we use phantasies derived from one person to understand the next. Children may accidentally call their teacher 'Mum' or their mother 'Miss'. This also provides possibilities for denial of unpleasant thoughts or feelings. It is simple in phantasy to substitute one person for another who shares some characteristic. A woman came for counselling because she felt that her husband no longer loved her. In her descriptions of daily life, it seemed that she 'knew' both that he did really love her, and at the same time was sure that he did not. Her own father had died when she was thirteen, the age her daughter was at the time. I suspected that her 'perception' of her husband's lack of love was a misattribution; she did not want to know that she feared that her father no longer loved her when he died. It was less painful to keep her idealised image of him and to see her husband as unloving. Unfortunately, this ultimately led to her own daughter being deprived of a parent as she had been herself. Not only did she misperceive the love of her husband, but she also actively created in her daughter feelings which came close to her own feelings when she was a child.

This is a form of denial helped along by a process we call 'projective identification'. Briefly, this involves feelings which cannot be tolerated being evoked in someone else, where their fate can be observed from a safer distance.

Counselling/Psychotherapy/ Psychoanalysis

In my own work as a counsellor, I find that these ideas make sense of ordinary, everyday interactions. Most of the people I see are not mentally ill. They bring to counselling the normal difficulties of life: struggles with parents, with children, with relationships, brought into focus by the symptoms of multiple sclerosis. But uncovering the phantasies behind ordinary difficulties can change their lives – and give me a privileged view of the human mind at work.

A mother told me that her son had suddenly lost interest in school. He talked of leaving and getting a job near home, when previously he had wanted to go to university and to travel. I knew that she had been very anxious when she was seriously ill a few weeks previously, and I wondered aloud if her son knew that her fears were now much reduced. I wondered if he wanted to stay at home to keep an eye on her; ultimately, to keep her alive. I suggested that he might have been too scared to look at her to see if she were better. She went back and spoke to him directly about her health, and afterwards, she said that it was as if the weight of the world had been lifted off his shoulders. A few days later he almost confessed to actually liking school. She said she felt guilty; she had enjoyed his solicitousness and had been thoughtless not to notice his anxiety about her. I suspected that the child was probably working quite hard to hide his worries from his mother, for fear of killing her with his own anxiety. Instead, he preferred to kill his ambitious self.

The link between a child's anxieties about his mother's health and his anxieties about school is an important one. So too is the realisation that a child's worry about his mother's health can feel like 'the weight of the world'. Often it is not necessary to know what the child's exact phantasies are, and parents have good reason not to like intruding on their children's privacy. But children can have quite unrealistic anxieties, based on partial information which has been eked out by the child's own phantasies. Phantasies are usually answers rather than questions, so children may simply 'know' that they will have to look after their mother alone if their father dies; or 'know' that they and their mother killed him by not loving him enough; or 'know' that it was their own bad behaviour which caused him to leave. It may simply not have occurred to children that other adults will come to their aid, or that they cannot have made their mother's MS worse by hitting her in play, or that telling her about their homesickness would not cause her damaging 'stress'.

Using the Ideas Outside the Consulting Room

Klein's ideas also make sense of behaviour outside the consulting room, though sharing one's interpretations may be more problematic there. A girl of twelve called over the fence to a boy of five. 'Would you like this?' she asked, holding out something. When the boy tried to take it, she snatched it away, laughing. She did this three more times. Then she turned to her friend in triumph, saying, 'He's so stupid, he fell for it four times!' Clearly the girl felt that the boy was stupid to hope that the world might be a friendly place. We can wonder whether she was making him feel something which she was afraid applied to her. In fact, she had reason to be anxious about whether the good things of life would be forever snatched away from her, just as she had begun to trust in their permanency. She must have thought that she was stupid to be taken in by her own hopes. Taking her game as a representation of anxieties (rather than just as evidence of childish sadism or cruelty) puts me in a position where I can at least think whether any of the adults in her life might be able to help her. In her case, there is a good chance that they will, but telling them my observation clearly has social implications.

Psychoanalysis

Psychoanalysts who work with patients five times a week can help with much deeper and more long-standing anxieties than those of us who see people once or twice a week. Holding anxieties alone over six days is quite different from holding them over the weekend, knowing that there will be five daily hours to work them through the next week.

I would like to show how one woman experienced powerful changes in her phantasies of a containing good object through several years of psychoanalysis. I am grateful for her permission to use this material. Ann went into analysis in her thirties, because professional and personal success had not brought her freedom from a constant sense of apprehension and anxiety. Her first dream in analysis was of a ruined house held up by scaffolding: the walls were open to the sky. She was clinging to a lampshade she had made herself, standing on a rickety ladder held by her father. Gradually the buildings in her dreams changed. They began to have roofs, though these leaked, and water poured down the internal walls. The buildings had precarious balconies and helpful or quarrelsome friends living in them. They were often dilapidated and awaiting repair. Sometimes Ann was hopeful, sometimes despairing about the amount of work needed to repair them. Gradually, over a period of years, the houses became firmer, more substantial. She still occasionally dreamed of ruins, but they were set in country parks, with grass growing over them. The final dream before she left analysis – feeling more secure than she had ever felt in her life – was of a large, substantial old house. Ann explained that 'it used to be a small convent, it had a history, but there were ordinary people having a meal on a big table in the garden, which was green and well-tended'.

Conclusion

The concept of unconscious phantasy was discovered by Freud and developed further by other analysts, in particular Melanie Klein and the analysts she inspired. Phantasies go on in our mind all the time without our knowing. Some are evident to other people; some are more concealed. These phantasies determine our interest in the world, our beliefs and assumptions, what attracts our attention and what we do with it. They are motivated by needs and desires. They deal with conflicts and anxieties in various ways by enabling us to work them through and test them against reality, both the reality of our own experience and the reality of the external world. We can also use phantasies to deny reality in various ways which are experienced as destructive; this destructiveness is itself often denied.

The idea that phantasies lie behind our every assumption, belief, thought, attitude, relationship and action may seem strange to begin with. We know that other people's beliefs are not always rational or sensible; that our own may not be based entirely on clear perception of reality may be harder to accept. What I like about the concept of phantasy is the way it allows both rationality and perception of reality their place. Phantasies may be perfectly rational and sensible; on the other hand, they may be based on simple misunderstandings arising from ignorance, and the whole structure of our thinking and behaviour will be affected – in a perfectly rational way. Many of the phantasies we use to understand ourselves and other people are fairly close to reality. These we can rely on; they will not let us down. Others are extremely primitive and unrealistic, yet they still allow us to get on with our lives in our own fashion.

Many of our normal phantasies, unrealistic but good enough to get us by in daily life, in fact create enormous amounts of anxiety. Others, created in an attempt to get rid of anxiety, deprive anxieties of the attention and thought necessary to allow them to resolve themselves peaceably, in their own good time. Understanding the way these phantasies work may allow us to find better ways of dealing with our own and others' anxieties.

Notes

1. *The Guardian*, 10 May 2000, p. 4. Amis, M., *Experience*, London: Jonathan Cape, 2000.

2. Freud, S., *The Standard Edition of the Complete Psychological Works of Sigmund Freud*, Vol. 10, trans. James Strachey, London: Hogarth Press and the Institute of Psychoanalysis, 1975, p. 190.

3. Freud, S., *The Standard Edition of the Complete Psychological Works of Sigmund Freud*, Vol. 1, trans. James Strachey, London: Hogarth Press and the Institute of Psychoanalysis, 1975, p. xxiv.

4. Freud, S., 'Studies in Hysteria', *The Standard Edition of the Complete Psychological Works of Sigmund Freud*, Vol. 2, trans. James Strachey, London: Hogarth Press and the Institute of Psychoanalysis, 1975, p. 157.

5. Freud, S., *The Interpretation of Dreams, The Standard Edition of the Complete Psychological Works of Sigmund Freud*, Vol. 4, trans. James Strachey, London: Hogarth Press and the Institute of Psychoanalysis, 1975, p. 259.

6. Freud, S., 'Studies in Hysteria', op. cit., p. 137.

7. Klein, M., 'The Development of a Child' (1921), in *Love, Guilt and Reparation and Other Works*

1921–45, The Writings of Melanie Klein, Vol. 1, London: Hogarth Press and the Institute of Psycho-analysis, 1975, p. 1.

8. Ibid., p. 35.

9. Ibid., p. 28.

10. Ibid., p. 42.

11. Ibid., p. 32.

12. Klein, M., 'The Role of the School in the Libidinal Development of the Child' (1923), in *Love, Guilt and Reparation and Other Works 1921–45, The Writings of Melanie Klein*, Vol. 1, London: Hogarth Press and the Institute of Psychoanalysis, 1975, p. 69.

13. Klein, M., 'The Development of a Child', op. cit., p. 42.

14. Orbach, S., *Fat is a Feminist Issue*, London: Paddington Press, 1978.

Further Reading

Bell, D., (ed.). *Psychoanalysis and Culture. A Kleinian Perspective*. London: Duckworth, Tavistock Clinic Series, 1999.

Caper, Robert. *Immaterial Facts: Freud's Discovery of Psychic Reality and Klein's Development of his Work*. London and New York: Routledge, 2000.

Caper, R. *A Mind of One's Own: A Kleinian View of Self and Object*. London and New York: Routledge, 1999.

Klein, M. *The Writings of Melanie Klein*, 4 vols. London: Hogarth Press and the Institute of Psychoanalysis, 1975.

Klein, M., Heimann, P., Isaacs, S., Riviere, J. (eds). *Developments in Psychoanalysis*. London: Hogarth Press and the Institute of Psychoanalysis, 1952.

Klein, M., Heimann, P., Money-Kyrle, R. (eds). *New Directions in Psychoanalysis*. London: Tavistock, 1955, 1971.

Menzies-Lyth, I. *Containing Anxieties in Institutions*. London: Free Association Books, 1988.

Segal, H. *Introduction to the Work of Melanie Klein*. London: Hogarth Press and the Institute of Psychoanalysis, 1973.

Segal, H. *The Work of Hanna Segal: A Kleinian Approach to Clinical Practice. Delusion and Artistic Creativity and other Psychoanalytic Essays.* London: Free Association Books, 1986.

Segal, J.C. *Phantasy in Everyday Life* (1985). Reprinted, London: Karnac Books, 1995; USA: Aronson, 1996.

Segal, Julia. *Melanie Klein: Key Figures in Counselling and Psychotherapy.* London: Sage Publications, 1992.

Spillius, E. *Melanie Klein Today*, 2 vols. London: Routledge, 1988.